```
J595.7                74-714
C75
Conklin
 Insects build their homes
```

DATE DUE			
SEP 5 '74	MAY 9 '85		
JUL 3 '74	JUL 9 1987		
AUG 23 '75	MAY 1 7 1990		
	NOV 8		
SEP 1 1 '75	JUN 8		
JUL 1 '76	MAR 2 8		
JUN 8 '78			
OCT 19			
JUN 26 '80			
OCT			
SEP 29			
APR 19 '84			

INSECTS BUILD THEIR HOMES

Other Books by Gladys Conklin

I LIKE CATERPILLARS
I LIKE BUTTERFLIES
WE LIKE BUGS
IF I WERE a BIRD
THE BUG CLUB BOOK
I CAUGHT a LIZARD
LUCKY LADYBUGS
WHEN INSECTS ARE BABIES
HOW INSECTS GROW
LITTLE APES
CHIMPANZEE ROAMS the FOREST
GIRAFFE LIVES in AFRICA
ELEPHANTS of AFRICA
TARANTULA: THE GIANT SPIDER

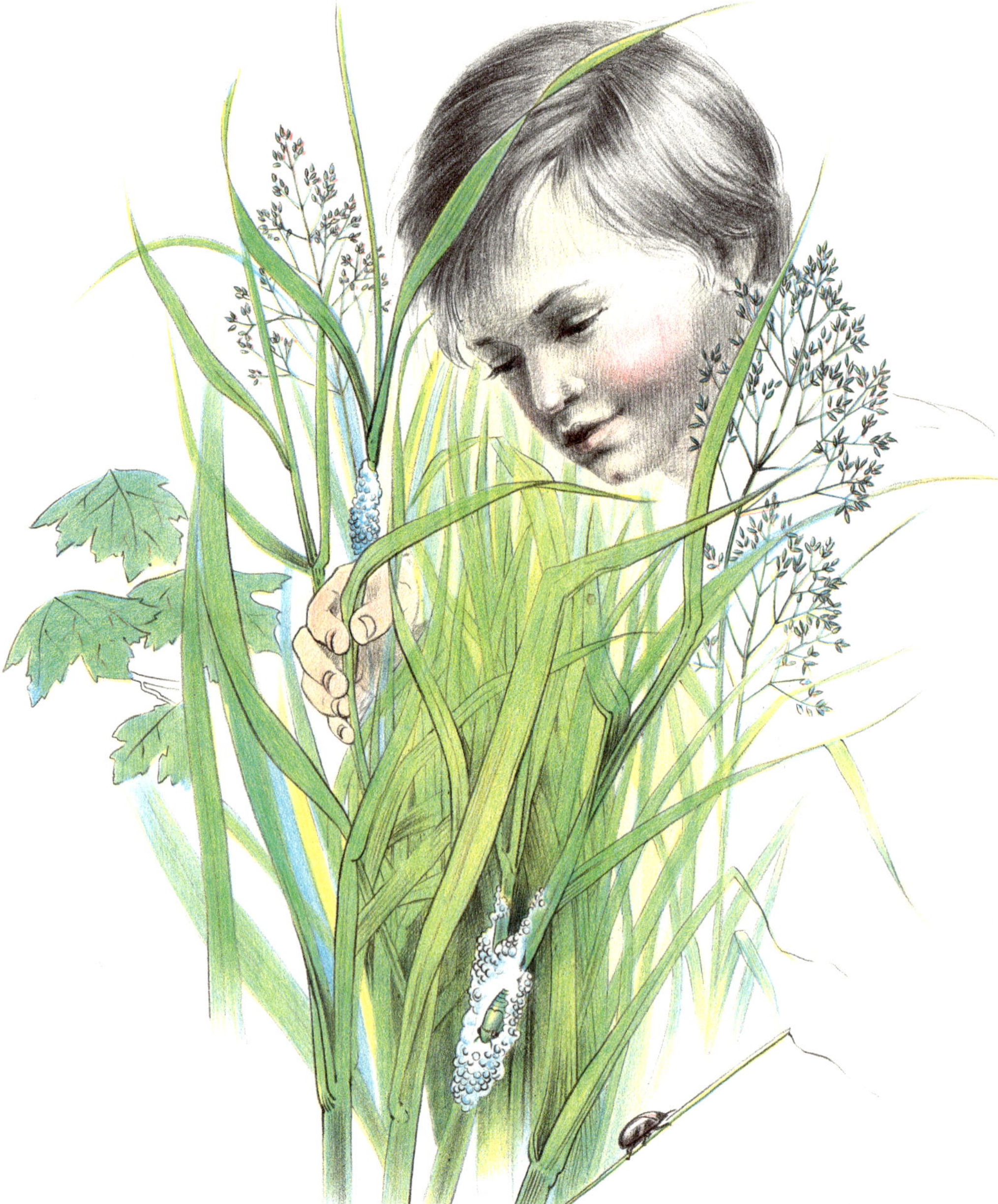

Gladys Conklin

INSECTS BUILD THEIR HOMES

Illustrations by Jean Zallinger

HOLIDAY HOUSE / NEW YORK

Text copyright © 1972 by Gladys Conklin
Illustrations copyright © 1972 by Jean Zallinger
All rights reserved
Printed in the United States of America
Library of Congress catalog card number: 72-75595
ISBN 0-8234-0207-X

For three special people:
Michael Christine John

Insects are all around us.
Many live on the bushes and trees.
Some hide in holes in the ground.
Others live in the water.

They are busy hammering and sawing, and cutting and digging. Some chew wood and make paper houses. Some spin silk and wrap up in silken cocoons. Others dig tunnels and live in the earth.

No one teaches insects how to build their homes. They know how to do the work the day they are born. We call this instinct.

The queen ant starts a new home under a rock. She digs out a small room and lays her first eggs.
When the eggs hatch, she has many workers to help her. They build a special room for the queen.
She spends all her time laying hundreds and hundreds of eggs.

The worker ants dig with their legs
and make long hallways.
They use their heads like bulldozers
and make many rooms.
They build large, cool nurseries for
the eggs. An ant nest is full of
busy ants—each doing his own job.

The larva, or young form, of the ant lion digs a hole in the sand. It uses its head like a shovel as it moves backward in a circle. A jerk of its head throws the sand out of the hole. The circle grows smaller and smaller until the hole is a V-shaped pit.

The larva lives at the bottom of the pit. You can see two sharp pincers sticking out of the sand. The larva feeds on ants and other small insects that fall into the pit. When it is time to change to an adult, the larva spins a round cocoon of silk and sand.

OPEN COCOON

A bumblebee chooses an old mouse nest for her nursery. She flies to the fields for pollen. At the same time she gathers nectar for honey. She returns to her nest and moistens the pollen with honey. She makes a paste to use as the floor of her first egg-cell.

HONEY POT

She lays about a dozen eggs in the cell.
She closes the top of the cell with
thin wax. Next she makes a small
honey pot out of wax. The honey will be
her food on rainy days. Her home
is finished and she does a curious thing
for an insect. She sits on her
egg-cell and keeps the eggs warm.

Kneel at the edge of a pond.
Look down to the bottom of the water.
You may see a small bundle of sticks
walking. A tiny head and six
little legs stick out at one end.
This is a caddis worm's home.
It is not really a worm, but a young insect.

There are many hungry insects in the water. A caddis worm is food for a dragonfly larva, or a water scorpion, or a diving beetle. A caddis worm builds its home for protection. It spins a roll of silk around its body. It fastens small twigs or bits of leaves to the silk. More and more twigs are added until the caddis worm is safe inside.

CHANUTE PUBLIC LIBRARY
102 South Lincoln
CHANUTE, KS. 66720

A black and white wasp is digging
a hole. It will be the home of her larva.
She carries the dirt out
of the hole in her forelegs. She digs
a long tunnel with a small room at
the end. This is the nursery of
a cicada killer.

The cicada killer flies to a tree to
find a cicada. She stings it and they
drop to the ground. The cicada doesn't
die but it can never move again.
The wasp turns the cicada over and
drags it between her legs. She takes
it to the small room in the tunnel.
She lays one egg on the body.
The cicada is fresh food for
the larva that hatches from the egg.

Look in the grass for bubbly balls of foam. In the center of the foam lives a little green insect. It is called a froghopper. It sucks juice from the grass to make the foam. Part of the juice is its food.

The froghopper, also called a spittlebug, works upside down. Its tail moves from side to side and the bubbles appear at the end. They pile up higher and higher. This strange home protects the soft body of the froghopper from the sun.
Stir the bubbles gently with a straw and you can see the bubble-maker.

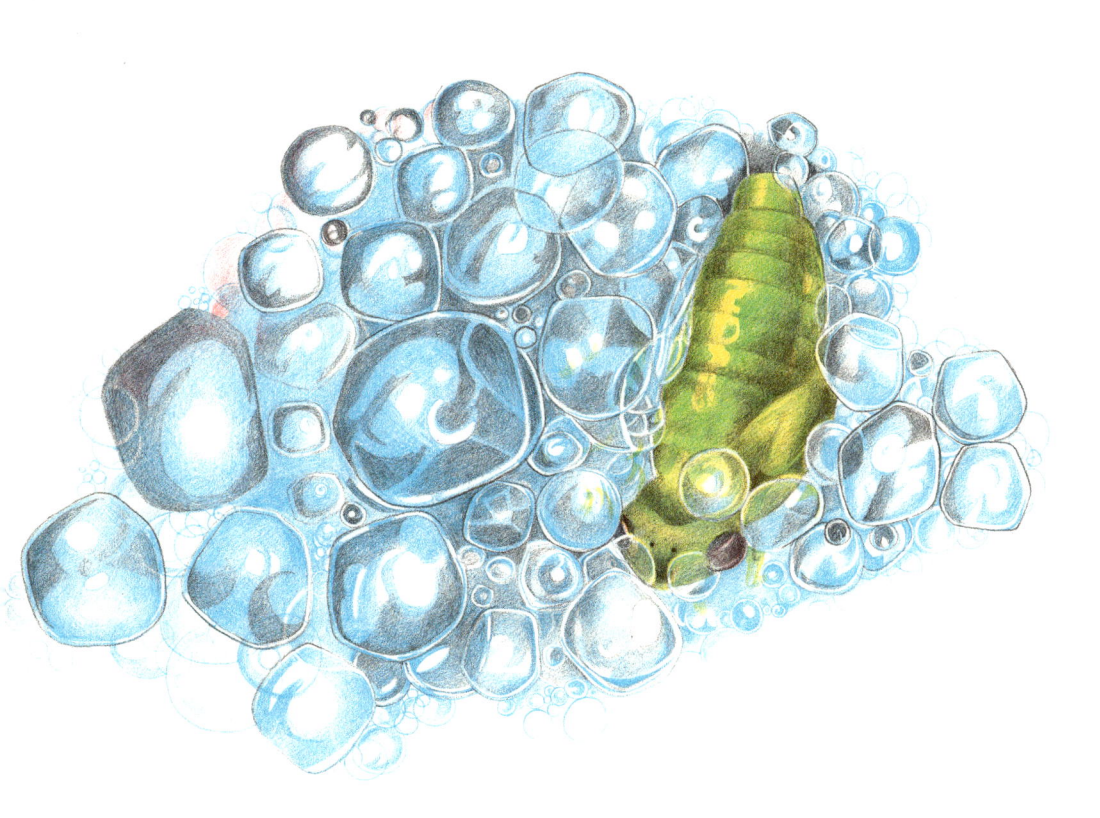

GOLDENROD GALL

The larva of the gallfly lives in a
special home made of a living plant.
The gallfly lays an egg
on a leaf or a soft stem. The egg
hatches and the small larva begins to eat.
The eating causes the gall to grow around it.
It grows larger as the larva grows bigger.

OAK GALL

The gall is also food for the larva.
The larva eats the soft insides
without destroying its home. Look for
galls on trees and plants. The
oak gall is one of the best known.
There are often many dozens of the small,
hard balls on one tree. Goldenrod also
has many galls. These are swellings
on the stems.

The giant water bug is one of our largest insects. He lives in ponds or in shallow water where cattails grow. He likes to fly and often buzzes around electric lights at night.

The female water bug picks
an odd place for her eggs. She lays them
on the back of the male.
She holds him and glues
her eggs on tightly. He can't fly with
eggs covering his wings. He stays in
the water and becomes a living home
for the eggs and the young water bugs.

You may hunt for a long time before you see a mole cricket. Mole crickets live in tunnels in the damp ground. Their wide, strong forefeet are fine for digging. Sometimes they leave their tunnels at night and fly around.

The female mole cricket digs a tunnel in a wet field. At the end of the tunnel she makes a special room. This is her egg room. She lays two or three hundred large yellow eggs. She stays to watch and guard them. When they hatch she stays with the young crickets until they can take care of themselves.

The mud dauber wasp builds a home for her young with mud. She works on the bank of a pond or under a dripping faucet. Watch her cut a small piece of mud with her jaws. She shapes it into a little ball and flies away. She may come to your porch or out to a barn. She presses the ball of mud against the rough wood. She pats it with her feet and her head until it is flat.

She gathers more mud and shapes it into little rings to make a cell. When a cell is finished, she darts off to find a spider. She stings it and carries it home. Using her head, she pushes it into the cell. She lays a single egg on the body and seals the nest. When the egg hatches, the young larva feeds on the fresh spider.

POLYPHEMUS

This caterpillar spins a thick cocoon between two or three leaves. It fastens silk threads to the leaves and pulls them together. It spins more silk and fastens the leaves to a branch.

For at least two days you can see the caterpillar working. Its head moves busily from side to side. It spins layer after layer of silk. When the cocoon is finished, the silvery color turns to a dark brown. The caterpillar wets it with a liquid. This gives the cocoon a hard, tough coat. It will be snug and warm in all the winter storms.

EGG CASE

EGG CASE

The praying mantis builds a strong egg case. She works upside down on a twig. Her body moves slowly back and forth. From the end of her body comes a frothy white foam. She lays some eggs, covers them with foam and lays some more.

She works without stopping.
She lays about three hundred eggs
in one egg case. When she covers
the last egg, she walks away.
She never looks around once.
The mantis builds well.
The eggs will be safe and warm in this home
even in winter rain and snow.

The tent caterpillar moth
lays her eggs on a branch of a tree.
She doesn't make a home for the
young caterpillars that hatch from
the eggs. They build their own home.

When the eggs hatch, the young caterpillars spin a little silk tent for their home. They leave it only when they go out to eat. As they move around, each caterpillar spins a silk thread for a path. They follow the path back to the tent. As the caterpillars grow, they spin bigger and bigger tents. They live together until they are ready to spin cocoons.

You may find a large green hornworm on tomato or tobacco plants. One day this caterpillar stops eating and digs down into the ground. It makes a small cave where it stays all winter.

In this cave the caterpillar sheds its skin for the last time. It changes into a large brown pupa with a small curved "handle." In the spring the pupa wiggles up out of the ground. It splits open and a gray moth crawls out. The moth has a tongue longer than its body. The tongue is protected inside the curved handle.

Tumblebugs live in the fields where there are cattle. You may see two black beetles rolling a small ball over the ground. This ball is made from the droppings of cows or sheep. It is food for the adult tumblebugs and also food for their young.

When the female is ready to lay eggs, she digs a small ditch. The male helps her roll a ball to this hole. She digs around the ball until it is buried in a small room. She pats the ball with her feet until one end is long and thin. It is now shaped like a pear. In the long narrow neck she lays one egg and then goes away. When the egg hatches, the young larva begins to eat its home.

Wherever you live there are insects
all around you. In the big cities
they are in the nearest park.
And you will find them
in your own back yard if anything
green is growing there. You may watch
insects at work if you move slowly
and quietly.

Insects do many strange things besides building homes. You may stand close to a flower and watch a bee gathering pollen. Or see a butterfly's long tongue uncurl and reach into a flower for a drink. Or see two ants meet on a path and touch antennas together to recognize each other.

No matter how many times you go to the park or out into the fields, there is always something new and exciting waiting for you to discover.